POCKET KIM WISDOM

POCKET KIM WISDOM

WITTY QUOTES
AND WISE WORDS FROM
KIM KARDASHIAN

hardie grant books

CONTENTS

KIM KARDASHIAN ON...

FAME
AND
SUCCESS

POCKET KIM WISDOM

'What is my talent?
Well, a bear can juggle and
stand on a ball and he's talented,
but he's not famous.
Do you know what I mean?'

– *Guardian*, 7th September 2012

FAME AND SUCCESS

'I'm an entrepreneur.
"Ambitious" is my middle name.'

— Cosmopolitan, 2nd October 2009

POCKET KIM WISDOM

'I love when people underestimate me and then become pleasantly surprised.'

– *Forbes*, 1st July 2010

FAME AND SUCCESS

'It's always funny to me when people say that I'm famous for being famous…I don't take offense to it at all.'

— *V Magazine*, September 2012

'Being on a reality show doesn't get the respect I feel it should.'

– *C Magazine*, August 2015

FAME AND SUCCESS

'I think it's more of a challenge for you to go on a reality show and get people to fall in love with you for being you.'

— Barbara Walters' 10 Most Fascinating People,
8th December 2011

'I have the control to put out what I want so even if I'm objectifying myself, I feel good about it.'

– San Francisco Commonwealth Club speech, 30th June 2015

FAME AND SUCCESS

'I always learn from my mistakes
but something like a photoshoot,
I never regret.'

– San Francisco Commonwealth Club speech,
30th June 2015

'The strangest thing I've ever read about myself online was that I was just obsessed with, like, killing raccoons and really weird animals.'

– *Paper*, 12th November 2014

FAME AND SUCCESS

'As long as they're talking
about me, honey.'

— *Keeping Up with the Kardashians*
season 2, episode 1

KIM KARDASHIAN ON...

MONEY

'When someone asks me,
"What do you do?"
under my breath I want to say,
"Ask my fucking bank account
what I do."'

— *LOVE Magazine*, February 2015

MONEY

[On Elizabeth Taylor's house]
'It was just so enchanting,
with a garden with really pretty
trellises and beautiful roses, but it
wasn't realistic for me to purchase.
It only had a one-car garage.'

— *Vogue*, April 2014

'I'm cheap about so many things…
I would say I am pretty frugal.'

— *MarketWatch*, 2nd July 2015

MONEY

'We've rented out Versailles.'

— *Keeping Up with the Kardashians*,
season 9, episode 18

KIM KARDASHIAN ON...

FAMILY

'There's a lot of baggage
that comes with us.
But it's like Louis Vuitton baggage:
you always want it.'

– *Keeping Up with the Kardashians*,
season 1, episode 1

FAMILY

'My mom and I have
always had this funny, weird,
cute competition.'

– *Rolling Stone*, 25th September 2014

'When you date one of us,
you kind of date the whole family.'

– Keeping Up with the Kardashians,
season 4, episode 1

FAMILY

'I think that there's the
Kim Kardashian brand and the
Kardashian brand…
But no matter what, we're family
and super close.'

— *Variety*, 24th April 2015

POCKET KIM WISDOM

[To her sister Khloe]
'You have a better, like, looking vagina than I thought.'

— *Keeping Up with the Kardashians*, season 5, episode 2

FAMILY

'For us, we've always been
about the business.'

– Daily Mail, 12th November 2014

'I rented my mom a monkey for the week because she had a syndrome where she missed children in the house.'

– *Late Show with David Letterman*,
1st October 2009

FAMILY

'We made a pact as a family
and said we would be
truly authentic because people
don't buy bullshit.'

— Marie Claire, December 2011

KIM KARDASHIAN ON...

MOTHERHOOD

'I think if I'm 40 and I don't have
any kids and I'm not married,
I would have a baby artificially
inseminated. I would feel like Mary —
like Jesus is my baby.'

Keeping Up with the Kardashians,
season 7, episode 5

MOTHERHOOD

[On pregnancy]
'I think God was doing this for
a reason. He was saying:
"Kim, you think you're so hot,
but look what I can do to you."'

– *Elle*, December 2014

POCKET KIM WISDOM

'I happen to hate the way I look in flats. It's really hard for me... And when I was pregnant, it was the hardest thing.'

– *Elle*, 4th June 2015

MOTHERHOOD

'Last pregnancy, I ate a doughnut a day, and I'm not going to do that this time.'

— Stylecaster, 4th June 2015

POCKET KIM WISDOM

'North doesn't typically wear pink…
She wears mauve or blush,
not, like, typical baby pink.'

– *The Sunday Times*, 15th February 2015

MOTHERHOOD

'The pregnancy, I wouldn't really wish
that upon anyone. Anyone.'

— *The Ellen DeGeneres Show*, 17th January 2014

'[My daughter is] very serious like her daddy… She just stares at you like, "Come on, I'm way smarter than you are right now." '

– KIIS 1065 Sydney radio interview, reported by *EntertainmentWise*, 21st November 2013

MOTHERHOOD

'My diaper bag is a Birkin
– a big one!'

– Marie Claire, 24th October 2014

KIM KARDASHIAN ON...

LOVE

'My decision to end my marriage
was such a risk to lose ratings
and lose my fan base.'

— *Oprah's Next Chapter*, 18th June 2012

LOVE

'Now I say, give it a good
six months before you commit.'

– *Cosmopolitan*, April 2013

'My relationship with
my husband, Kanye, really
changed everything.'

— *CNN*, September 2015

LOVE

'I have this best friend who understands me and helps me through all my tough experiences.'

— *Cosmopolitan*, April 2013

[On Kanye]
'We're kind of obsessed
with each other.'

– *Vogue Australia*, February 2015

LOVE

'[Kanye's] the most romantic
guy I have ever met.
He's better than any movie
or romantic novel.'

— *The Ellen DeGeneres Show*, 17th January 2014

'So many other people I know have gotten married on TV and it has worked out amazing for them. William and Kate got married on TV.'

– Guardian, 7th September 2012

LOVE

'I believe in love, always.'

— *People*, 16th December 2011

KIM KARDASHIAN ON...

STYLE AND IMAGE

POCKET KIM WISDOM

'Back in the day, I thought
I had the best style. I look back at
outfits and I'm like, mortified.'

— *CNN*, September 2015

STYLE AND IMAGE

'I feel really blessed because
I genuinely love the
process of getting my hair
and make-up done.'

– Into the Gloss, February 2015

'I love my husband's opinion,
so I always ask his opinion on
everything and he always helps
me put together my looks.'

– *CNN*, September 2015

STYLE AND IMAGE

'Kanye always says,
"Dress sexier!"
He's always the most encouraging.'

— LOVE Magazine, February 2015

'I only just started wearing
underwear a month ago,
and I never wore underwear
until then.'

– *LOVE Magazine*, February 2015

STYLE AND IMAGE

'I always pee all over my Spanx, it's a disaster. They aren't crotchless enough!'

– LOVE Magazine, February 2015

POCKET KIM WISDOM

'In recent years, I'm, like,
too cool for duck face, so that
doesn't happen.'

— NPR, 13th June 2015

STYLE AND IMAGE

'The key to a good selfie
is lighting. If you're not feeling
yourself, make it darker.'

– San Francisco Commonwealth Club speech,
30th June 2015

'I'm definitely not getting naked or taking my clothes off ever again.'

— *Kourtney and Kim Take New York*,
seaon 1, episode 2

STYLE AND IMAGE

'I like nudity.'

– *LOVE Magazine*, February 2015

'Shopping online is like,
the greatest invention of life.'

— *Kourtney and Kim Take Miami*,
season 3, episode 10

STYLE AND IMAGE

'I have the hairiest forehead you could
ever imagine.'

– People, 4th March 2015

'I hate when women wear the wrong foundation colour.
It might be the worst thing on the planet.'

— *Toronto Sun*, 20th October 2010

STYLE AND IMAGE

'My entire body is hairless.'

– *Allure*, September 2010

'I love where my eyebrows
are going right now.'

— *People*, 4th March 2015

STYLE AND IMAGE

'I'm obsessed with contouring.
My nose is a completely different
nose because of contouring.'

– *Rolling Stone*, 16th July 2015

'Know your angles. I like
up to down and there you go –
a perfect selfie.'

– San Francisco Commonwealth Club speech,
30th June 2015

STYLE AND IMAGE

'There's nothing we can do
that's not documented,
so why not look your best,
and amazing?'

— *Paper*, 12th November 2014

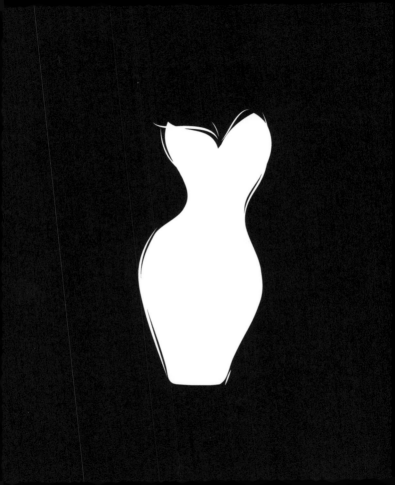

KIM KARDASHIAN ON...

HER
ASSETS

'I don't have anything against my butt. I've got a lot to thank it for, perhaps.'

– GQ, October 2014

HER ASSETS

'It's like an Armenian thing.
It runs in the family and we're all
really curvy. So I thank my roots
for giving me a big butt!'

– *Alan Carr: Chatty Man*, 18th May 2012

'I don't get why everyone
is always going on about my butt.
I'm Armenian. It's normal.'

– *Harper's Bazaar*, 2nd May 2014

HER ASSETS

'Even when I was a little girl…
all my friends would be like,
"Oh, my god, your butt's so big."
And I'd say, "I love it." '

– *Cosmopolitan UK*, May 2011

'There's constant interest in my bottom!'

— *StarPulse*, 10th September 2009

HER ASSETS

'Actually my butt is not that big.'

– *LOVE* magazine, February 2015

KIM KARDASHIAN ON...
HERSELF

'I've never claimed
to be anything that I'm not.'

– V Magazine, September 2012

HERSELF

'I am so much smarter than
I'm portrayed.'

— Rolling Stone, 16th July 2015

'I guess people would call me
a feminist.'

– San Francisco Commonwealth Club speech,
30th June 2015

HERSELF

'I buy myself a gift every year,
so this year I bought everything
I wanted.'

– CBS San Francisco, 17th October 2010

'I'm so mature now. I'm a grown-up version of myself.'

— *W*, November 2010

HERSELF

'I live my life on a reality show…
Yes, it is ridiculous, but it's all fun.'

— AdWeek, 2nd March 2015

'It's crazy anyone should assume that, just because you're in the spotlight, you're flawless.'

– *Cosmopolitan UK*, May 2011

'[I took] my first selfie in 1984.'

— AdWeek, 2nd March 2015

POCKET KIM WISDOM

'It's really hard to live in
a world where there's so many
people judging you.'

– Vogue Australia, February 2015

HERSELF

'I always wanted to be famous.'

– *Vogue Australia*, February 2015

'I like sharing my world with people.'

— *Vogue Australia*, February 2015

'Everything is better with a K.
Klassy with a K, hahaha!'

– *Harper's Bazaar*, 9th February 2011

Pocket Kim Wisdom

First published in 2016 by Hardie Grant Books, an imprint of Hardie Grant Publishing

Hardie Grant Books (UK)
52–54 Southwark Street
London SE1 1UN

Hardie Grant Books (Australia)
Ground Floor, Building 1
658 Church Street
Melbourne, VIC 3121

hardiegrantbooks.com

British Library Cataloguing-in-Publication Data. A catalogue
record for this book is available from the British Library.

ISBN: 978-1-78488-060-6

Publisher: Kate Pollard
Senior Editor: Kajal Mistry
Editorial Assistant: Hannah Roberts
Art Direction: Ami Smithson, www.cabinlondon.co.uk
Cover Illustration © Kayci Wheatley, www.kayciwheatley.com
Cover background © iStockPhoto
Images on pages 1, 2, 3, 6, 18, 24, 34, 74 © Shutterstock
Images on pages 6, 44, 54, 82 © iStockPhoto
Colour Reproduction by p2d

Printed and bound at Toppan Leefung, DongGuan City, China